THE DOG

ELLA EARLE

summersdale

THE DOG

Summersdale Publishers Ltd
46 West Street
Chichester
West Sussex
PO19 1RP
UK

www.summersdale.com

Printed and bound in China

ISBN: 978-1-84953-143-6

Substantial discounts on bulk quantities of Summersdale books are available to corporations, professional associations and other organisations. For details telephone Summersdale Publishers on (+44-1243-771107), fax (+44-1243-786300) or email (nicky@summersdale.com).

To:..

From:..

DOG, n. A subsidiary deity designed to catch the overflow and surplus of the world's worship.

Ambrose Bierce, *The Devil's Dictionary*

Few delights can equal
the mere presence
of one whom we
trust utterly.

George MacDonald

If your dog thinks you're the greatest person in the world, don't seek a second opinion.

Jim Fiebig

The average dog is a nicer person than the average person.

Andy Rooney

Dogs lead a nice life.
You never see a dog
with a wristwatch.

George Carlin

Whoever loveth me, loveth my hound.

Thomas More

Money can buy you a
fine dog, but only love
can make him
wag his tail.

Kinky Friedman

Even the tiniest poodle or chihuahua is still a wolf at heart.

Dorothy Hinshaw Patent

Animals are such agreeable friends – they ask no questions, they pass no criticisms.

George Eliot

Hardly any animal can look as deeply disappointed as a dog to whom one says 'No'.

Jeffrey Moussaieff Masson

Dogs are my favourite people.

Richard Dean Anderson

Friendship is a single soul dwelling in two bodies.

Aristotle

There is no psychiatrist in the world like a puppy licking your face.

Bern Williams

If dogs talked, one of them would be president by now.

Dean Koontz

Character is higher than intellect.

Ralph Waldo Emerson

A door is what a dog is perpetually on the wrong side of.

Ogden Nash

Dogs are a habit, I think.

Elizabeth Bowen

The biggest dog has been a pup.

Joaquin Miller

The better I get to know men, the more I find myself loving dogs.

Charles de Gaulle

The pug is living proof that God has a sense of humour.

Margo Kaufman

Happiness is
a warm puppy.

Charles M. Schulz

We don't stop playing
because we grow old;
we grow old because we
stop playing.

George Bernard Shaw

Fox-terriers are born
with about four times
as much original sin in
them as other dogs.

Jerome K. Jerome

The dog is a gentleman;
I hope to go to his
heaven, not man's.

Mark Twain

I read the *Odyssey* because it was the story of a man who returned home... and was recognised only by his dog.

Guillermo C. Infante

From a dog's point of view, his master is an elongated and abnormally cunning dog.

Mabel Louise Robinson

No day is so bad it can't be fixed with a nap.

Carrie Snow

The language of friendship is not words but meanings.

Henry David Thoreau

There is no friendship, no love, like that of the parent for the child.

Henry Ward Beecher

If animals could speak, the dog would be a blundering outspoken fellow.

Mark Twain

Dalmatians are not only superior to other dogs, they are like all dogs, infinitely less stupid than men.

Eugene O'Neill

Why not be oneself? That is the whole secret of a successful appearance. If one is a greyhound, why try to look like a Pekingese?

Edith Sitwell

No matter how little
money and how few
possessions you own,
having a dog makes
you rich.

Louis Sabin

If ever the world's diplomats and arms negotiators learn the spaniel gaze, there will be peace on earth.

Larry Shook

Love is the emotion that
a woman feels always
for a poodle dog and
sometimes for a man.

George Jean Nathan

In times of joy, all of us wished we possessed a tail we could wag.

W. H. Auden

All we need to make us really happy is something to be enthusiastic about.

Charles Kingsley

They motivate us to
play, be affectionate,
seek adventure
and be loyal.

Tom Hayden

If I have any beliefs
about immortality, it is
that certain dogs I have
known will go to heaven,
and very, very
few persons.

James Thurber

They serve us in return for scraps. It is without a doubt the best deal man has ever made.

Roger Caras

Laziness is nothing more than the habit of resting before you get tired.

Jules Renard

To sit with a dog on a hillside on a glorious afternoon is to be back in Eden...

Milan Kundera

Women and cats will do
as they please, and men
and dogs should relax
and get used to the idea.

Robert A. Heirlein

Dogs are better than human beings, because they know but do not tell.

Emily Dickinson

To the world you may be just one person, but to one person you may be the world.

Brandi Snyder

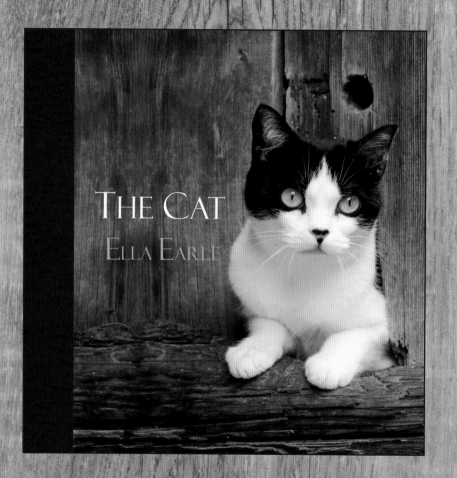

THE CAT

ELLA EARLE

THE CAT

ELLA EARLE

ISBN: 978-1-84953-142-9   Hardback   £6.99

*The cat could very well be man's best friend
but would never stoop to admitting it.*

Doug Larson

Combining gorgeous and characterful photographs
with witty and heart-warming quotations, this
enchanting celebration of our feline friends
is a must-have for any cat lover.